Contents

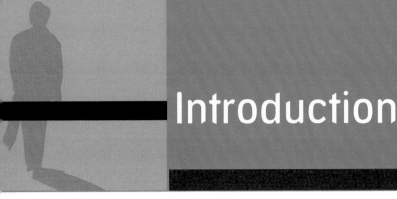

Introduction

From stopping would-be assassins to preventing terrorist attacks, the Federal Bureau of Investigation (FBI) has always been on the scene, ensuring the safety of the American people. They've busted rings of organized crime. They've tracked down spies. They've even uncovered evidence that led to a U.S. president's resignation. Behind the many successes, however, how in the world does the FBI solve these crimes?

The answer is simple. FBI agents are highly skilled. These agents have years of special training to their credit. Many can read and speak foreign languages. Others have strong military backgrounds. Together, the agents use their know-how to enforce the nation's laws. In this book, we'll examine some of the most famous cases from FBI files. We'll also learn about the history, and the future, of this crucial agency.

Some people imagine shootouts when they think about the FBI. However, this bureau is at its best when it gathers bits of vital information.

Chapter One

What Is the FBI?

The FBI is one of the United States government's main law enforcement branches. However, the FBI isn't like your local or state police. They are only interested in federal crimes. These are crimes that happen across more than one state, or involve national security. Federal crimes can include kidnapping, espionage (or spying), and terrorism.

How It Began

President Theodore Roosevelt believed the national government should play a role in preventing crime. In 1908, President Roosevelt formed a group of Special Agents. These agents were part of the Department of Justice. Up until 1908, many people felt that city and state law enforcement groups could handle any crime. However, the United States was

President Theodore Roosevelt knew that many criminals would never be brought to justice without the help of the federal government.

going through drastic changes. More states were joining the Union. The nation's population was growing by leaps and bounds. The nature of crime was changing, too. The nation needed an investigative team that could solve large-scale crimes. The group would eventually be given the authority to solve crimes that crossed state lines.

Gangster Days

In the early 1920s, a new type of crime was on the rise. It was called organized crime, or gangsterism. Gangsterism involved illegal activities carried out by a large circle of criminals. These criminals worked together across many states. The gangs committed armed robberies and sold stolen goods. They also murdered members of rival gangs. Thanks to Special Agents, many infamous gangsters were put behind bars. Al "Scarface" Capone was one of the nation's most notorious gangsters. He committed many crimes. Many murders were carried out by his order. Special Agents believed that Capone ordered the

Al Capone skirted the law for years. Finally, though, Scarface had his day in court—thanks to Special Agents.

St. Valentine's Day Massacre of 1929. On that day, in Chicago, members of Capone's gang executed seven rival gang members. Yet Capone remained out of the law's reach.

Capone was living in Miami, Florida. Capone's lawyers said he couldn't travel to Chicago to testify in any court cases. They claimed he was too sick to travel. Special Agents looked into the lawyers' claim. They discovered it was a lie. In fact, Capone did a *lot* of traveling. He went to racetracks. He also took luxury cruises and plane flights. For someone who was too ill to travel, Capone was seeing a lot of sights! Eventually, the law caught up to Al Capone. He was finally sent to jail—not for murder, but for not paying his taxes!

Another infamous gangster that Special Agents pursued was Baby Face Nelson. When Special Agent Samuel P. Cowley tried to arrest Nelson, there was a shoot-out. Both Nelson and Cowley were killed in the gunfight.

The Man at the Top

The value of Special Agents became clear after the key role they played in battling organized crime. Much praise was heaped on J. Edgar Hoover, the bureau's director. There is no doubt that Hoover's leadership shaped the FBI. No one questioned his dedication. Hoover's policies, however, had many critics. Hoover investigated the personal and professional lives of many citizens. The FBI kept thick files on the activities of politicians and other famous Americans. After World War II, many Americans began to wonder if he had been given too much power. This caused some to become fearful of Hoover.

CLASSIFIED INFORMATION

In July 1935, the FBI was given its official name. Ever since, they've had their hands full with tough cases. At any given moment, the FBI is on the lookout for 12,000 fugitives!

Spies Among Us

Fear—of a different kind—was what pushed Hoover to keep those secret files in the first place. Many U.S. citizens and politicians, including Hoover, believed that communism posed a threat to the nation's security. FBI agents suspected that spies were trading away national secrets to communist countries. As a result, the FBI investigated people and organizations that had links to espionage activities. This period of fear and suspicion became known as the Red Scare. During this time, many Americans were accused of being spies. Some of the accused were later found guilty of betraying their country. However, others had been falsely accused. For them, the Red Scare caused much sorrow and embarrassment.

Trouble at Home

The 1960s and 1970s presented new challenges to the bureau. The assassinations of President John F. Kennedy and Dr. Martin Luther King Jr. kept the country on edge. It also kept the bureau busy. The

J. Edgar Hoover (right), shown here with President John F. Kennedy, led the FBI from 1924 until his death in 1972.

FBI aided in the investigations of these crimes. On America's streets, many citizens were protesting the Vietnam War. These people strongly believed that the U.S. should end the war. While most protests were peaceful, some turned violent. FBI agents arrested those who used violence or carried weapons to make their point.

To complicate matters, other authorities had begun to investigate the FBI itself. They found that Hoover's bureau was involved in some illegal activity of its own. Still, for the most part, FBI agents did their duty well. In 1972, they investigated an unusual break-in. The break-in had taken place at the Democratic National Committee (DNC) head-quarters at the Watergate Hotel in Washington, D.C. Agents found illegal listening devices installed in the DNC's hotel room.

After months of investigation, blame for the break-in led back to President Richard Nixon. At the time, President Nixon was running for reelection. The FBI discovered he was also spying on his political rivals. The case became known as Watergate. President Nixon resigned, or quit, his presidency because of the Watergate scandal.

The FBI Today

Since its early days, the FBI has taken on many roles. The bureau now tackles drug trafficking and international crimes. It investigates terrorist acts committed on both U.S. and foreign soil. Today, the FBI employs about 11,400 Special Agents and 16,400 Professional Support Personnel. These employees work out of fifty-six field offices and forty-four Legal Attaché offices. A Legal Attaché office is one that is located in a foreign country. Constructed in 1932, the FBI Technical Laboratory, in Washington, D.C., has become one of the world's leading forensics centers.

When the FBI started the Watergate investigation, they would have never guessed that the trail of the crime would lead back to President Richard Nixon.

Chapter Two

Special Agents

Those who dream of joining the FBI must meet several requirements. Applicants must be U.S. citizens. They must be between the ages of twenty-three and thirty-seven. They should be in top physical shape. They must take drug-screening and lie-detector tests. Also, they must agree to a full background check. Background checks can take up to four months to finish. All of these tests help ensure that applicants meet the FBI's high standards.

First Assignment: Hitting the Books

Special Agents fulfill many duties. They collect evidence from crime scenes. They interview suspects and witnesses to these crimes. They also learn how to identify and study clues. Because their job requires quick thinking, Special Agents must have a good education. All agents graduate from a

Before Special Agents work in the field, they must complete months of training.

four-year college. Here are the areas in which most
Special Agents have degrees:

- Computer Science
- Physical Sciences
- Accounting
- Health Care
- Engineering
- Foreign Language
- Law
- Education

Because they deal with criminals, Special Agents must learn to make split-second decisions. To sharpen their skills, agents simulate dangerous situations.

Special Agent Training

Those hired as FBI Special Agents won't be assigned to tough cases right away. They must first report to the FBI Academy in Quantico, Virginia. There, they begin a sixteen-week training program. At Quantico, agents must pass numerous exams. They are tested on subjects such as ethics, organized and violent crime, and national security. Agents also undergo intensive physical training. This training helps improve their body strength and stamina. FBI agents receive instruction in using handguns, shotguns, and

CLASSIFIED INFORMATION

Want a taste of FBI work? Apply for an internship! To qualify, you must be a junior or senior in college. You must have good grades in school. You must also live near the FBI's Washington, D.C., headquarters, or be willing to move nearby.

sub-machine guns. After finishing these tough weeks, the agents graduate. They then move on to their first cases.

The FBI Laboratory

Agents at the FBI Technical Laboratory are always examining and searching evidence. Lab technicians carry out more than a million examinations each year. These examinations may involve looking at DNA, fingerprints, shoeprints, and tire tracks. Laboratory agents examine all the evidence given to them. Any piece of evidence might help crack a case.

Laboratory agents come from all walks of life. They have one thing in common: expertise in a certain field. That field may include computer science, finance, or even photography. A chemistry expert might identify toxic substances recovered from a crime scene. The chemist, for example, might find traces of the toxic compound cyanide. Later, at the FBI Laboratory, he or she might determine that this cyanide was used in an attempted murder.

The clues to solving crimes can be found anywhere. Imagine a suspect drives away from a crime scene. The side of the getaway car scrapes against a telephone pole. Agents would take samples of any

Those who commit crimes try to cover all their tracks. However, FBI Laboratory agents pride themselves on using the smallest clues—such as dandruff and fingerprints—to bring culprits to justice.

car paint found on or near that pole. Forensic experts would then examine these paint samples in the FBI Laboratory. Based on the results, they might be able to figure out exactly what kind of car the suspect was driving.

Other Opportunities

The FBI headquarters is made up of many other divisions. These include the National Security and Counterterrorism Divisions and the Office of the Director. Each division needs its own lawyers, accountants, and scientists. Divisions also hire people with military intelligence experience. These workers help make sure that FBI operations run smoothly.

Top Ten List

For over fifty years, the FBI has released its Ten Most Wanted Fugitives list. The list may be the FBI's most well-known feature. The list displays a recent photo of the fugitive, along with his or her full name. By displaying criminals' faces, the list makes it easier for the public to spot criminals. Since its creation, 475 fugitives have been placed on the list. As of June 2002, 445 of those fugitives have been located. It's people like you that have helped. The general public has aided FBI agents in finding 145 of these dangerous men and women.

The idea for the list first occurred in 1949. A reporter asked the FBI for the names of the criminals they were having the toughest time capturing. By publishing the names, the public could help bring these people to justice. The reporter's article was a huge success. J. Edgar Hoover decided to keep the list going. In 1950, Thomas James Holden became the first fugitive to appear on the list. Holden had committed three murders in Chicago. He then dashed across state lines to escape authorities. An Oregon resident recognized Holden from the list. FBI agents soon captured him.

Chapter Three

On the Scene

In the movies, murder weapons are often left at the crime scene. This makes it easy to find the culprit. In real life, crimes are not so simply solved. The scenes where real crimes occur take much longer to search than the fictional crimes of movie sets.

Prepare

When FBI agents get assigned to an investigation, they first decide how to work together as a team. Everyone is given a job based on experience and training. The team then picks a leader. This leader will be in charge of making important decisions during the search.

The group tries to learn as much as possible about the crime before they even reach the scene. They talk

It's important to take photographs at a crime scene. Pictures can help refresh agents' memories about the details of a crime. Photos can also serve as vital evidence if the case is presented in court.

with people who were there when the crime happened. They also speak to other law enforcement
officials who might have visited the crime scene
already. Sometimes the team needs to bring a search
warrant to the scene. A search warrant is a legal doc-
ument written by a local court. It gives investigators
permission to search a crime scene.

When FBI agents reach a crime scene, it's their
duty to search the area with a combination of
caution, speed, and thoroughness. They must also
keep their emotions in check at all times.

Visit the Scene

When the team reaches the crime scene, they try to figure out if anything has changed since the crime was committed. For example, have other people walked past the area since the crime happened? If the crime happened in a room of a house or office, was any of the furniture moved? Does it seem that the desk drawers have been disturbed?

Sometimes a crime scene might involve violence. There may be a dead body, or the remains of one, at the scene. Each member of the team must be prepared to find anything. They have to keep their emotions in check, even if what they see is very disturbing.

Gather Evidence

To make sure that every corner of the crime scene is searched, the team uses a specific search pattern. For instance, they may search the room from right to left. Or they might start from the center and spiral out. All team members wear gloves. This way, they won't leave fingerprints. Evidence is gathered carefully. The search team first gathers evidence, such as blood, that could change or break down over time. The team then gathers other items, such as wallets or keys. During the investigation, the team scans for hidden objects. They also search all entrances and exits to the crime scene.

Tell a Story

While gathering evidence, the FBI team writes a story of what happened. This story describes each known fact of the case being investigated. It mentions the date, time, and location of the crime. The story also describes the condition of the crime scene. Was it raining? Was the search done during the day or at night? Does it look as if the crime happened recently? Could it have been committed weeks or months ago? Team members also take photographs and draw sketches of the crime scene. They add these things to the written story.

To solve tough mysteries, FBI agents may put themselves in harm's way. This agent is about to gather clues inside a building that has been exposed to a deadly anthrax virus.

Before Leaving

At the end of the search, the team goes over the crime's details once more. They make sure the notes, photographs, and sketches they've collected are complete. When the team finishes, the leader hands over the information to other FBI members or the local police. This is called the release of the crime scene.

Recent Crime Scenes

Kenbom

It was mid-morning when pedestrians felt the impact. On August 7, 1998, a bomb rocked the U.S. Embassy in Nairobi, Kenya, in Africa. The blast ripped apart the embassy floors and damaged many neighboring buildings. The explosion claimed the lives of 212 people, while wounding 4,500 more. Twelve of the dead were Americans.

Within hours, the FBI was on the case. The case was given the code name Kenbom (short for "Kenya bombing"). Nearly 500 agents were flown to Nairobi. They began their investigation quickly, often working to the point of exhaustion. Some agents spoke with witnesses and the local police force. Others collected evidence from the crime scene. They searched the area for remains of the explosives. They gathered any clue that would help them bring the criminals to justice.

Along the way, they followed leads and asked questions. What kind of bomb was capable of doing

FBI agents are always on call at a time of crisis. Hundreds of them were quickly flown to Africa after the U.S. Embassy in Kenya was bombed.

this? How many criminals were involved? Why would they commit this horrible crime? Finally, where could they be found?

The agents' thorough investigation paid off. So far, it has led to the convictions of four criminals involved in the bombing. Investigators learned that these criminals had ties to the terrorist organization known as Al Qaeda. However, the agents' work is not yet done. Thirteen other suspects—including Al Qaeda's leader, Usama bin Laden—remain at large.

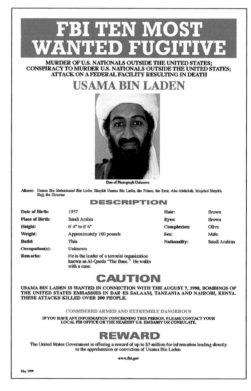

FBI TEN MOST WANTED FUGITIVE

MURDER OF U.S. NATIONALS OUTSIDE THE UNITED STATES;
CONSPIRACY TO MURDER U.S. NATIONALS OUTSIDE THE UNITED STATES;
ATTACK ON A FEDERAL FACILITY RESULTING IN DEATH

USAMA BIN LADEN

Date of Photograph Unknown

Aliases: Usama Bin Mohamrnad Bin Ladin, Shaykh Usama Bin Ladin, the Prince, the Emir, Abu Abdallah, Mojahid Shaykh, Hajj, the Director

DESCRIPTION

Date of Birth:	1957	Hair:	Brown
Place of Birth:	Saudi Arabia	Eyes:	Brown
Height:	6' 4" to 6' 6"	Complexion:	Olive
Weight:	Approximately 160 pounds	Sex:	Male
Build:	Thin	Nationality:	Saudi Arabian
Occupation(s):	Unknown		
Remarks:	He is the leader of a terrorist organization known as Al-Qaeda "The Base." He walks with a cane.		

CAUTION

USAMA BIN LADEN IS WANTED IN CONNECTION WITH THE AUGUST 7, 1998, BOMBINGS OF THE UNITED STATES EMBASSIES IN DAR ES SALAAM, TANZANIA AND NAIROBI, KENYA. THESE ATTACKS KILLED OVER 200 PEOPLE.

CONSIDERED ARMED AND EXTREMELY DANGEROUS

IF YOU HAVE ANY INFORMATION CONCERNING THIS PERSON, PLEASE CONTACT YOUR LOCAL FBI OFFICE OR THE NEAREST U.S. EMBASSY OR CONSULATE.

REWARD

The United States Government is offering a reward of up to $5 million for information leading directly to the apprehension or conviction of Usama Bin Laden.

www.fbi.gov

May 1999

The FBI Ten Most Wanted List is designed to capture the vilest criminals—such as Usama bin Laden—and ensure they never strike again.

World Trade Center — The First Attack

In 1993, a bomb exploded in the basement of the World Trade Center in New York City. The explosion killed six people and injured thousands more. About 300 FBI agents joined forces with the New York City Police Department to run the investigation. FBI Special Agents uncovered crucial clues. They found parts of a car, which they learned was used to carry the bomb. The FBI Laboratory pieced the car fragments together and studied them. They found a code number that matched the number on a van stolen from a car rental agency in New Jersey. FBI agents eventually traced the van to the last man who rented it. This man became the first suspect in the case. He was quickly arrested. Within a month, the crime search at the World Trade Center was completed. Three more people were arrested. A year later, the four people were accused of thirty-eight crimes. They went on trial, and a jury convicted them all. The defendants were each sentenced to 240 years in prison.

Chapter Four

The Future of the FBI

What Next?

Cyber Crime

We certainly live in the computer age. Banks, telephone companies, and credit card services all use the Internet. For these businesses, the Internet provides a fast, easy way to track records. For a cybercrook, however, the Internet is another way to break the law. Instead of robbing a bank by gunpoint, cybercrooks steal money by breaking into a bank's computer system. Catching cybercriminals is a tricky task. The FBI must work hard to understand how these criminals hack into computer systems. Agents will also need to figure out what electronic clues the e-criminals leave behind.

Quiet as a mouse: Using computers, crooked cybercriminals try to rob unsuspecting victims of millions of dollars, without firing a single bullet!

Identity Theft

Most people use certain personal information every day. This information includes social security and credit card account numbers. These numbers are important to our everyday lives. They are used to buy things, travel on airplanes, and get jobs. What if this information falls into the wrong hands? Criminals try to use innocent peoples' identities to commit serious crimes. Identity theft goes hand-in-hand with cybercrimes. That's because much of our personal information can be found on the Internet. Criminals can use a stolen identity to buy costly things, such as a house. Some criminals use stolen identities to commit other crimes. When this happens, innocent people are accused of committing crimes. Each year, over half a million Americans have their identities stolen. To fight identity theft, more secure computer systems will need to be put in place.

Terrorism

FBI agents caught the criminals that bombed the World Trade Center in 1993. However, this was not enough to prevent a second attack on the buildings.

On September 11, 2001, Americans woke up to an unspeakable horror: a series of violent terrorist acts committed on U.S. soil.

37

On September 11, 2001, terrorists hijacked four planes. They flew two of these planes into the World Trade Center. One plane was flown into the Pentagon in Washington, D.C. The fourth plane crashed in a field in Pennsylvania. Over 3,000 innocent people were killed in these attacks. Their

CLASSIFIED INFORMATION

The Ten Most Wanted Fugitives list has led to the arrest of many hardened criminals. Sometimes, though, it just catches clowns. In 1965, agents arrested a criminal named Leslie Douglas Ashley in Atlanta, Georgia. Ashley had a strange way of escaping justice. He got a job as a clown in a traveling carnival! Luckily, a fellow carnival worker saw through Ashley's grease-paint and wig. This worker recognized Ashley as a fugitive and called the FBI. Ashley's days in the Big Top were through for good!

deaths will haunt people for years. The attacks may change the way people in America live forever.

The attacks have affected the FBI's role, too. In May 2002, FBI Director Robert Mueller put an important plan into effect. Mueller created a special unit of the FBI. This unit will be located in Washington, D.C. Its resources will be solely devoted to fighting terrorism. The unit will provide agents with a way to share leads and tips. For instance, if Special Agents in different cities receive the same terrorist threat, they will inform the D.C. unit. In the past, an agent in Minneapolis, Minnesota, would have had no way of knowing that another agent in Phoenix, Arizona, had heard about the same threat. This new unit will help the FBI respond to terrorism with greater accuracy and speed than ever before.

Taking Things Too Far?

Crimes of the future will demand a lot from FBI agents. Agents will need to pay extra attention to the backgrounds of suspected criminals. Yet agents will also need to be fair. Sometimes, investigating a suspected criminal can lead to problems. This became clear after the September 11, 2001, terrorist attacks.

After these attacks, the FBI detained hundreds of people for questioning. Many of the detainees had ties to Middle Eastern nations such as Saudi Arabia and Egypt. The FBI held these people for a reason. They did it because the terrorists they were looking for had come from these countries. Yet many of the detainees had nothing to do with the attacks. For them, weeks of questioning caused stress and anxiety. Some were required to spend months away from loved ones. Catching actual criminals is a tough duty. Yet the FBI knows that it must balance the needs of the law with the rights of the people.

Building a Better Tomorrow

In spite of setbacks, the FBI's number one goal is still clear. That goal is to protect the people of the United States. To succeed, agents must learn new skills.

In the days following September 11, 2001, U.S. leaders made it clear that the nation's need for FBI resources was stronger than ever.

They must ask the right questions. They must continue to pursue the truth. Yet they must also be sure they don't mistreat or harm innocents during their search.

The nature of crime has changed in recent years. The FBI no longer just catches spies or breaks up organized crime. Criminals can now break the law from anywhere in the world. They can steal your name and identity. They can also threaten the places where you work and live.

As long as the FBI keeps changing with the times, it will keep succeeding. Special Agents will be able to foil the toughest threats to national security. Of course, there's one mission FBI agents should never change. That mission? To be fair to, and respectful of, the people they protect.

By sharing more information and clues with one another, FBI Special Agents won't be afraid of walking into dangerous situations in their fight against terrorism.

New Words

crime scene the place where a crime happened

culprit someone charged with, or guilty of, a crime

cybercrimes crimes that take place over the Internet

detained to have held in a cell, usually for questioning

detainees people placed in a holding cell
for questioning

espionage the use of spies to learn military secrets of
other countries

evidence material that can be used in a court to prove
that something is true

forensics using knowledge of science to solve crimes

fugitive a person who runs or attempts to escape from
the law

notorious well-known for causing trouble or
committing crimes

terrorism the use of violence to reach a goal

For Further Reading

Campbell, Andrea. *Forensic Science: Evidence, Clues, and Investigation.* Broomall, PA: Chelsea House Publishers, 1999.

DeAngelis, Gina. *Cyber Crimes.* Broomall, PA: Chelsea House Publishers, 1999.

Douglas, John E. *John Douglas's Guide to Careers in the FBI.* New York: Kaplan, 1998.

January, Brendan. *The FBI.* Danbury, CT: Franklin Watts, 2002.

Resources

Web Sites

Official FBI Web Site
www.fbi.gov

FBI Laboratory
www.fbi.gov/hq/lab/labhome.htm

FBI Youth
A fact-filled introduction to the Federal Bureau of Investigation.
www.fbi.gov/kids/6th12th/6th12th.htm

U.S. Government Web Sites for Kids (service of the U.S. Government Printing Office)
bensguide.gpo.gov/subject.html

Index

Index

About the Author

Sheela Ramaprian holds a Master of Fine Arts degree in Creative Writing. She works as a technical writer in the software industry. Like law enforcement agencies, many information technology companies must learn how to respond to crime over the Internet.